I0471421

Can I Borrow Yes you can - A Guide To Declutter Your Finances

How To Borrow, Save And Invest For Your Future

By: Darren Wiley

[Enter ISBN-13 9781483946214]

TABLE OF CONTENTS

Darren Wiley

PUBLISHERS NOTES
Disclaimer

Paperback Edition 2013

Manufactured in the United States of America

DEDICATION

This book is dedicated to Shanique who provided her expertise on debt management to help to get this book put together.

CHAPTER 1- START BY DECLUTTERING YOUR FINANCES - HOW TO DECLUTTER YOUR FINANCES

Whether you're managing an individual budget or one for your whole family, there is nothing quite as unsettling to modern life in general as having your finances in disarray. Debt and overwhelming financial obligations may seem like they sprung up out of nowhere, but there are simple steps toward decluttering your finances.

When we think of the financial clutter concept, we consider it a figure of speech, but the truth is; conceptual clutter is often accompanied by very real, physical clutter. How many times do we struggle to find an important document, or sort through statements? Important and documents that are hard to replace like insurance, birth certificates and property titles should be kept in a lock or deposit box. A filing cabinet would be ideal to keep the remaining documents but if you don't have one, document folders can do just fine. You should have one for inactive papers you nonetheless need to keep, like tax records, and another for active papers that require action, like invoices.

The first step in financial decluttering is to gain all possible information on the status of your finances, and keep that flow of information manageable. Most financial institutions and utility companies offer the possibility of switching to electronic statements that will keep you from procrastinating on sorting through your junk mail to open the truly important letters. Then of course, there is the task of sorting through the already accumulated mail and filing it appropriately, getting older statements into an archive and unpaid bills in a visible place (that hopefully, won't be covered by physical clutter).

Once that information is gained, it's time to identify which standing monthly bills you must honor in full, every single month. These will most likely be utility bills, which for the most part, have an automatic bill pay sign up option. Set it up to save your time and possibly, worries and money on late fees and stress from cut-off warnings when you simply forgot the bill or didn't prioritize the money for your basic needs.

Converting your financial management to an electronic format is also a step to consider. There are online budget and document management tools that are safe, and most of all, are accessible from any computer. Physical papers can be misplaced or damaged, so a digital copy can save time and concerns.

Consider also, renegotiating and consolidating your bills. Many companies have Internet, cable and phone bundles that can save you not only money, but time and possible mishaps when you have several invoices taken care of at once. Also, try contacting providers of non-essential services for free upgrades or cost reductions. Attempting to get a company to match a competitor's offer can score you a free upgrade, and cutting a few non-essential frills, like a few channels from your cable service, can reduce your monthly expenses.

Now that you have automated your bills, you should do the same for your savings. Having an economic cushion for family emergencies is not a luxury, but a necessity, and you should treat the safety of yourself and your loved ones with as much importance as keeping the power on your home. Nearly all bank accounts offer automated money transfers from your checking account to your savings. These can be high interest, or even save you from overdraft fees. The same can be done for retirement savings, which can be done for example, when signing up for the company's 401(k).

Dealing with debt will require a multifaceted approach that is nonetheless, quite simple at its core. The first thing to do is so obvious most people don't consider it as a first step – stop accumulating debt. Day to day expenses should come off of a debit card and the credit card should be left at home, preferably in a lock-box. Debt mismanagement comes not from the lack of money, but from the lack of balance between money made and money spent. The opposite of a debt-ridden life is not financial wealth, but rather, lack of debt. In practical terms, this means, you don't have to work more, but you do need to start living within your realistic means. This may signify that you'll have to cut down on luxuries, but have a stress-free life, which we can all agree, is a priceless state of mind. Unsubscribing from electronic and snail mail offers, discounts and catalogs is vital for keeping the onslaught of spending temptation at bay and reducing the amount of communication to sift through.

For the debt you do have already, consider re-negotiations or consolidation. Contacting the companies that own your debt with goodwill to repay what you owe often results in payment re-negotiations that you can handle. Most creditors are more interested in being paid realistically than sticking to the original payment plan. If however, you have an excessive number of high-interest rate debts, consider consolidating them all with a loan. This option should be well studied as it simplifies your current finances at the cost of a possibly higher expense over time.

If you already have, or are interested in investments as a way to save for retirement, you can cut time and effort by outsourcing the research and portfolio handling portion of your stocks and bonds. The great majority of mutual fund companies offer customized portfolios that adjust your retirement savings investments according to the amount of time you have until retirement. These "lifestyle funds" diversify and allocate your stock and bond options for you, effectively decluttering your finances.

CHAPTER 2- HOW DOES YOUR CREDIT SCORE AFFECT HOW YOU CAN BORROW MONEY

Business is business. Your credit score does not rely on democratic factors but on objective financial data. There are people who do not take into consideration the requirements that they need to show in order to be granted a loan. Here are the basics of how your credit score affects how you can borrow money:

There are different percentages that determine how much money you can borrow. It is good to know these criteria in order to determine how they measure your ability to pay.

Out of total of 100%, 10% of credit score criteria are reviewed from the current credit that a person has already established. This includes installments that you are now currently paying and as well as mortgages.

Another 10% is also considered if you have existing credit. These include recent purchases that may or may not involve long-term investments.

A record of your credit history is also reviewed. This is considered to have a higher importance, so 15% is graded when you have a good payment history.

Credit investigators also check the ratio of your debit and credit. 30% is the highest grade score for a perfect debit-credit ratio.

Lastly, the most important factor to determine how you score is the history of payments which includes activity for more than a month.

The important thing to remember is to clear out any records of late payments in order to have higher score. Even if these factors are somewhat related, each one is important to achieve high loans.

Keep old credit accounts, choose to cancel new ones. This is the most common behavior of consumers. More often than not, old credit accounts are cancelled especially if a huge loan has just been completely paid. Many people often apply for new ones because there are better offers or payments are more flexible. Remember that old credit accounts make up for 15% of the entire credit score. The older a credit account that is in good standing is the better chances of getting an increased score.

Properties are sure way to get a better score. This is already a general knowledge. For those who are new to loans and investments, it is good to know that properties are great way to offer as collateral. Lots and lands increase in price over time unlike other investments like vehicles or gadgets that lessen in amount as they depreciate. If you do not own any property as of the moment, make sure to live at an address for at least one year. This also shows that you are stable and able to maintain your finances.

Consider household bills, even those with cheap amounts. Credit companies also investigate the little finances that are paid on a regular basis. This may be as small as a local phone bill however they are helpful to determine how you score. Consider paying bills before the due date. This is to ensure that you will have a stable credit standing and create an impression that you are financially secure.

Never spend on a credit card to its maximum amount. One thing that credit investigators review is the way a consumer spends. Credit companies often get an impression of bad finances if there are several instances when a credit card is continuously used up to its spending limit. Credit cards should also be thought of as an option to use only in case of sudden expenses. This is why a maxed out amount gives hints that you may be managing your money poorly.

Check out the offers from credit card companies. These companies extend their marketing strategy in the most outrageous ways so that people can be lured to impulsively apply for one. While it is true that having a credit card is one way to create a credit score, certain cards may not help. For example, a credit card company will offer a promise of no increase in rate when a good is purchased. The deceiving part is when they suddenly increase a rate just because of your credit score.

The bottom line of this tip is to stick with your old credit card. First, the transaction and payment history can be a great way to increase your credit score. Second, the familiarity of its terms and conditions is an advantage. If you have ever experienced being deceived by these credit card companies, there are ways to make a complaint. It is important to contact the lender as soon as possible. There are many reasons why an increase in a credit card rate is done. Examples of these include: overdue payments, debt history, and many more.

If you are currently in debt, reduce your costs. This is possible since many companies would prefer to provide you an option to pay rather than keep you in debt. To lessen the amount of your credit card loan, you can contact the company directly. They are equipped with many options for you to pay debts in a more convenient way. If this does not go well, you can get free debt advice from a credit organization. These organizations offer free advice via phone, chat, email, or even personal meetings.

To make personal loans easier to manage, you should also contact the lender directly. If you are able to shift a current loan to another, it may offer more flexible terms of payment. The risk of doing this is that you may be paying more without noticing the increase. It is inevitable for companies to increase loan prices in relevance to the length of your payment terms.

As you can see, there are several factors that influence how credit agencies determine your overall credit score. To determine how much you can borrow, take note of even the smallest details that can affect your credit rating. With a little effort on your part as well as seeking the advice of others, you can achieve the ideal credit score you need in just a short amount of time. With that sorted how can you get the loan you need?

CHAPTER 3- THE DIFFERENT WAYS YOU CAN BORROW MONEY

What Is An Overdraft?

An overdraft occurs when a client of a bank withdraws more money from his account than he actually has in the account. Banks will often use the term "not sufficient funds" to refer to an overdraft, and people sometimes refer to overdrafts as "bouncing checks."

Often, if there is almost enough money in the account to cover the withdrawal, the bank will cover the overdraft and allow the withdrawal to go through. Typically the bank will charge a fee of approximately $20 to $30 for covering an overdraft; however, there is no legal restriction on the amount of fees or fines the bank may charge. In some cases, the bank will also charge interest on the amount which it has in effect loaned its client in covering the overdrawn transaction.

Darren Wiley

Many banks offer overdraft protection, which allows clients to overdraw their bank accounts. Banks charge monthly fees for overdraft protection, and usually set a predetermined limit to the amount that a client may overdraw. Sometimes banks will link overdraft protection to a client's savings account, and will automatically transfer money from the savings account to the checking account to cover the overdraft.

Overdrafts often occur because the client hasn't kept his account balanced, and doesn't know how much money is actually in the account at the time of the transaction resulting in an overdraft. One common scenario that produces overdrafts happens when a client forgets about an automatic withdrawal or payment he has scheduled. An overdraft can also occur when the client makes a deposit but doesn't know that the bank has placed a hold on it; in this case, the client may believe he has sufficient funds to cover the transaction. Sometimes bank fees of which the client is unaware trigger an overdraft, or a deposit made by the client bounces without the client being aware of it.

At times, overdrafts occur due to error on the part of the bank or, more frequently, on the part of a merchant who withdraws an incorrect amount of money from the client's account. When this occurs, banks will sometimes refund any fines or fees charged for the overdraft.

The best protection against overdrafts is to keep your check register up to date and balanced at all times, and to check the account balance and transactions to make sure all deposits are being properly credited.

What Is A Credit Card?

A credit card is a plastic card that is a bit smaller than a card in a playing deck of cards. It has a magnetic strip on the back of it and has sixteen numbers on the front of it along with your name and expiration date. You will use this card the very same way that cash is used except this card is much safer than carrying a lot of money on you. Carrying money isn't safe as it used to be so many people carry a credit card. Use the card just like you would use money. It will pay for all of your purchases and you never have to use cash at all. If this card would ever get stolen, it's easily stopped and the person that stole your credit card would not be allowed to use it to make any purchases. It would be harder for the person to try to use your credit card to gain cash as well.

You would go to a bank and apply for a credit card. In doing so you would give the bank your personal details and give them your name and address and let the bank know where you work, how much income you make as this will decide exactly how much money you would be able to use on your credit card. You would now have a credit card to use instead of using cash and the dollar amount is given by your personal information.

Darren Wiley

If the bank that you were applying to for a credit card gave you $10,000 in credit that would mean that they are giving you $10,000 to spend as you would like. You wouldn't see the money but you would have their credit card allowing you up to $10,000 to spend. You will have to pay them back with interest. It is safe to have a credit card but then it may get costly if you are not careful of your very own spending habits.

You take this credit card with you and while shopping and if you wanted to make a purchase you would tell the cashier you are paying for your merchandise with a credit card. There would be a small machine that you will take your credit card and swipe it into that machine and pull it out. The card will have all your information on it and allow for you to pay for what you just bought without using cash. It's that simple to use the card. These cards will be handy all over plus you can use it to buy an airplane ticket to go on vacation. The money is there for your use.

What Is A Personal Loan?

Personal loans are usually given by banks for different reasons. Sometimes, business owners may use a personal loan to get started on their business. The amount of the personal loan varies depending on how eligible one may be. These loans are also good for hardships as well. The bank may require you to pay them back monthly or give you some time before making your first payment. In order to apply for your personal loan you will have to take some time to talk with a personal banker and see if it is the right choice for you. He or she will suggest how to apply and you can even apply there in person.

Depending on your eligibility, there may be a high or low interest rate with your personal loan. Some loans have really good interest rates depending on the bank you go through. Others may have a high interest rate which will be applied to your payments when you start paying the bank back. For you to be eligible most banks require you to be between the ages of 21-60 years old if you are employed by a company. If you are self employed, you must be between the ages of 25-65 years old. They also have different guidelines to go by such as the amount of professional experience one has. This could be how long you have been in your job. They usually want you to have at least two years of this experience plus one year in your current occupation. Financial conditions also affect your eligibility for a loan. This will determine how much interest you will have on your repayment.

The branch manager of the bank will help you to negotiate the best option possible. If the interest rate of the personal loan seems high you might be able to talk them down. Sometimes if you apply at where you are already banking they can be lenient. If you have had loans with the bank in the past you may increase your chances of getting a personal loan if you have had a good repayment history. Personal loan applications may take some time to process according to the bank's procedures.

What Is A Mortgage?

Many people have certain dreams they want to attain in life. One of the most common is to own a home. Although there are a few options to achieving this goal, a mortgage is the most common road traveled. Buying a home without debt, which means having a giant savings account, is not plausible for most. A mortgage is probably the largest debt that a person will ever have. This being said, it is important to know the facts before you jump in with both feet.

A mortgage is a loan that is used to finance the purchase of a home. Your home becomes the collateral for the loan. A mortgage is usually dispersed from a bank or other lending company. When you enter into the mortgage, you are also entering to a legal contract with the lender.

A mortgage's terms are spread over a 15 or 30 year repayment schedule. The time period varies and is dependent upon the amount owed. Month payments are made to the lending company to cover costs of the loan to buy your home. Included in this payment are principal, interest and often, taxes and insurance as well. The principal of the loan is simply the money you borrowed to buy your house. Interest is normally written in percentage and is what the bank charges to issue you the loan. It can vary depending upon credit score and length of loan terms.

Generally, the longer your repayment schedule, the more interest you will pay. Taxes are built in to help home owners budget the healthy charges for living within the community. Taxes are used to build schools, improve roads and better the community. Depending if you live in a city or rural area, taxes can range from a small amount to several thousands of dollars yearly and are determined by your city or county government. All of these factors come together to determine your final monthly payment and is referred to as the PITI.

If you are ready to find a home to buy, please be informed. This is a big step and can adversely affect those that do not see its seriousness. Failure to pay your mortgage can result in loss of your property without equity or refund of payments.

What Is A Business Loan?

A business loan is money a bank or other lending organization gives to a business or a person starting a business that must be paid back according to the terms of the contract. The contract for the business loan will contain information on the amount of money being borrowed, how much time is being given for paying back the loan, the amount of the monthly payments, and the interest rate.

Getting a Business Loan

Many entrepreneurs or new businesses need to avail themselves of a business loan in order to get started if they don't have enough of their own monies to begin their business venture. Another reason a person or company may need a business loan is so that they can upgrade or expand their existing business.

Depending on the reason for getting a business loan, the bank may need to see a copy of a proposed business plan or may need some sort of collateral to back the loan in case the recipient were to default on the loan. Loan recipients must also qualify for taking out the loan based on their credit report and other obligations.

The amount of interest for a business loan depends on the current prime rate that the Federal Reserve Bank sets for the day the loan is approved, along with the recipients credit record, collateral vs. a signature loan, the amount of political climate and the risk the bank is taking on in order to give the loan. It may also depend on things like the bank's operating costs, wages and salaries of bank employees, processing fees, and the bank's overhead costs.

Paying Back a Business Loan

When the payment date is set for a business loan depends on why the business or individual is getting the loan. For instance, loans for land, equipment or other tangible items could generate a payback schedule based on a specific number of equal payments with a possible larger payment at the end term of the loan.

But if it is used for something that doesn't have any collateral, then there is more risk for the bank, so the payment schedule may be shorter and the interest rate could be higher.

The bottom line is that a business loan is something that a person or company applies for in order to raise funding so that they can pay for starting up, expanding or otherwise getting things for their business needs.

CHAPTER 4- HOW TO BORROW TO INVEST - THE RIGHT WAY

The decision to borrow money for the purpose of investing is an important one and if not done the right way, will yield devastating consequences. Use the following advice to put yourself in the most advantageous position.

Should You Consider Borrowing To Invest?

Borrowing to make investments should be done under the right conditions. Think about the following criteria and how closely it describes your situation, to determine if it's right for you:

Your income consists of varied and reliable sources, such as a salary from a secure position.

You have additional funds from which to draw upon should the market experience significant decline.

The tax bracket you normally find yourself in is high enough to provide you with reduced borrowing costs.

You are clear about the risks involved and comfortable with unpredictable results or are otherwise able to withstand the potential loss.

Analyzing the Risk Factors

Investing naturally comes with risk, no matter what funds you are drawing from to buy, however; the risk increases considerably if you are borrowing to do so. No matter how lucrative an investment appears to be or how certain you might be of its value, borrowing to invest nearly always compromises your position.

When you borrow to invest, you are more vulnerable to market spikes and the consequences of a falling market can devastate your overall position.

You run the risk of losing 100% on your investment and still owing on the money you borrowed.

The larger the amount you are borrowing, the higher your risk for loss is.

Failure to diversify on the investment further increases the potential volatility of your position; the investment that favors one particular company or industry is particularly dangerous.

Preparing to Borrow for Investment

Once you've analyzed the risks and qualified yourself for borrowing to invest, it's vital that you strengthen your position and sharpen your vision. Borrowing to invest the right way involves calculated risk and careful analysis.

Understand your financial health right now; what you owe, income(s), expenses and how the potential loss from borrowing to invest would influence your current standing.

Have clear and realistic goals to follow and don't deviate from them.

Know your limits and how risk works cooperatively with your goals.

Avoid any further action within your portfolio until these investments clear. Regardless of the outcome, you will have loans to repay and the need to reanalyze your position before considering any other major changes to your financial position.

Selecting Your Method of Borrowing

The different ways you can borrow the money you need to invest are as important as the calculated risk you are taking; consider them carefully, weighing the potential impact of gains or losses on your investment both short and long-term.

Obtaining a loan or credit line- Your bank may see fit to lend you the amount of money your investment requires (which is a good sign) and the interest you pay in return varies according to your total amount borrowed, length of the loan, collateral, credit rating and other specific terms. Be certain you can meet them in the event your investment sours.

Using your home equity or mortgage leveraging- Provided the investment takes care of your borrowed position and makes money for you, this scenario is obviously favorable, however; should the endeavor fail, your loss will be considerable.

Buying on margin- Borrowing directly from the brokerage firm to cover the cost of your investments carries more risk and leaves you in the unenviable position of possibly losing more than the amount of your initial investment. Proceed with margin buying carefully.

Short selling (with a margin account)- Borrowing shares you expect to significantly go lower in price can provide you with the necessary investment capital, but again the risks are great; you may find yourself owing more back to the investment firm than you invested and clearly hindered.

Your Best Bets for Borrowing

The smarter you borrow, the better your investment position, no matter what goes down (or up). Put as much thought into your borrowing as you do your investments. Know the process well and how to work it to your advantage.

Avoid borrowing over a set limit- It may take you a decade to break even on a sour investment scenario and the greater the amount borrowed, the longer the leveling period will be. Despite optimism on your risk, always consider the potentials involved with loss when determining your borrowing limit.

Understand transaction fees- Knowing which asset class to go with can improve your investment position and your best bet isn't always the one you are most familiar with; read the fine print to assess all variables and minimize the cost associated with borrowing fees.

Declutter Your Finances

Know the best tax scenario- Your investments may benefit from different filing positions and angles on claims, but it's a tricky situation to optimize; consult with a good source to educate yourself in this area or consider outsourcing brain power to get the greatest tax value.

Weigh short-term risk vs. long-term returns- Setting goals helps you manage the course of action you take, based on expectations and speculations. Your borrowing position is strengthened by time and patience.

Borrowing to invest is an adventure fraught with many emotions and a lot of learning. Use this information to take some of the lows out of the process and make informed, intelligent and successful decisions.

CHAPTER 5- WHY BANKRUPTCY CAN BE AN ISSUE FOR ANYONE

It can be easy to judge someone for having to file for bankruptcy. Most think that the action comes as a result of a failed business venture or being too poor to afford one's bills. An individual might assume that a person spent paychecks uncontrollably or was careless and lazy when it came to paying bills promptly. While this may be the case for a few, the truth is that bankruptcy can be an issue for anyone. There are several circumstances that may be wholly out of a person's control that causes bankruptcy to be the only practical option.

Sheer ignorance about bankruptcy can actually contribute to falling prey to the same financial situation. Quite simply, it results from insurmountable debt that becomes too overwhelming to pay. When debt has spiraled out of control beyond an individual's ability to personally repay it, bankruptcy is often the only solution. The fact is that debt is an issue everyone must deal with at some point in time.

Consider the life goals of the average person: graduate high school, buy a car, go to college, graduate college, get married, have children, own a home, and finally retire. Along the way, a person may or may not venture into pursuing a Master's Degree or Doctorate or even launching one's own business. Every one of these milestones costs a significant deal of money, and chances are that every person intends to pursue at least a couple of the goals listed.

Unless an individual is in the miniscule percentile of the population that is born into money or wins the lottery, he or she will need to apply for a number of loans throughout a lifetime. Even with scrimping and saving, most people must take out a loan in order to purchase a vehicle. A monthly car payment accounts for a significant portion of a paycheck. For the purchase of a used car the average loan term is about 64 months or more than five years, with a payment of $350. For new cars, the monthly payment is $485 over a 62-month term.

Most dream of pursuing higher education and earning a college degree in order to establish a good career and financial security in the future. Again, this goal more often than not requires a considerable loan. By the time the average student graduates, he has acquired $26,600 of debt. These are just two of the most common loans among the majority of individuals.

Besides large loans, bankruptcy looms in the distance for a number of other responsibilities common amongst the majority of individuals. Everyone struggles with similar life responsibilities that lead to the same kinds of debts: things like credit cards, mortgages, rent, and medical bills. It is easy to become busy and begin to miss payments. Overwhelming debt coupled with even one or two late payments can negatively affect one's credit and begin to contribute to a downward spiral of debt accumulation that eventually leads to bankruptcy.

But even the rich succumb to financial complications and are not exempt from bankruptcy. Even Donald Trump has had multiple issues with bankruptcy. In fact, it is quite common to read or hear of bankruptcy in media gossip. In cases with the wealthy, filing for bankruptcy may result from poor management of money, bad investments, or a simple habit of overspending and carelessness with the budget. For example, Trump recently filed for bankruptcy over a casino business venture for the second time. However, it is a fact that creditors are more likely to impose bankruptcy on the rich than on the poor.

Essentially, the wealthy often struggle with bankruptcy for the same reason everyone else does: because the amount they owe exceeds the total value of their assets. This is the essence of bankruptcy and it is a situation that remains the same across all demographics. Oftentimes, because of their considerable incomes, the wealthy are able to correct their poor financial choices and renegotiate outstanding debt. But sometimes even the rich are unable to do this, opting instead to file bankruptcy which allows them to repay debt over a period of 3 to 5 years.

The economy has been in a poor state for several years. The recent presidential elections highlighted this grave subject for weeks, revealing the enormous national debt, which affects all U.S. residents through mediums such as taxes and increased prices. These added financial burdens often serve as the proverbial "straw that broke the camel's back," forcing even the most financially responsible to file for bankruptcy.

The worsening economy makes it possible for anyone to be let go from their job and difficult to find a new one. Debt begins to accumulate. Even if a person is fortunate enough to find work, the new pay may not match the old salary. If an individual is unable to make the necessary spending adjustments to make ends meet debt quickly spirals out of control.

While anyone is susceptible to bankruptcy issues and anyone can apply for bankruptcy relief, the fact is that not everyone will qualify for it. Without legal representation, it can be difficult to even make it past the first phase of the process. This is because the requirements have been adjusted to meet the needs of only those who truly need it. For this reason, it is important for those struggling with overwhelming debt to get legal assistance in order to get the help they need.

CHAPTER 6- HOW TO IMPROVE YOUR CREDIT SCORE

When considering how to improve your credit score, analyzing the systematic steps that guarantee positive credit profile growth is of the utmost importance. First and foremost, at the most rudimentary level, maintaining good credit has to do with simply paying bills on time. Essentially, the credit bureaus want to see that you have established a pattern of being able to make good; when it comes to strict financial deadlines or promises. With that said, major credit reporting agencies are looking at a particular score, which translates to your collective credit report card, given a 7 to 10 year period.

Paying on time encompasses a range of options including paying a bill in full, or making down payments, to say, a number like 10 percent, ranging to a 30 percent balance- to-credit line availability ratio. If you are able to maintain these types of balances, your credit is well on its way to a stellar score and you will continue to improve your credit score.

Credit can be made stronger by keeping debt low, thereby ensuring against financial overextension. This truly is an important factor in the credit rating procedure in so far that the credit finance industry is aiming to protect against financial overextension by monitoring things such as how many credit cards an applicant has at one time in addition to how many credit cards that person has applied for given a relative time span. Even applying for new lines of credit may give future financial institutions the idea that you are headed for financial instability, which could in turn result in a lowered credit rating.

Considering the nuances of paying on time, one can improve on good credit by breaking into the elite financial category of a stellar credit, scoring somewhere in the neighborhood of 750. For example, considering two different scenarios - the person pays the full monthly balance, every month, or up to 30 percent of total balance each month. So, comparatively, if one typically falls into the category of situation b; in which the person pays only the bare minimum of the required monthly balance, thereby leaving no gap at all between available credit and used credit, the score can be improved on immediately by starting anew pattern of paying down the debt at a higher monthly payment rate. Once the maxed out credit begins to show signs that it is on the track to being paid down, the credit is sure to show signs of improvement.

It is no secret that credit card companies and financial lending institutions are concerned with the idea of being paid back and how that will happen, this is the bread and butter of the financial lending. And, in line with this reasoning, part of the reason for a standard credit application or credit inquiry, is to establish how much verifiable income one has and generally has access to. Overextension is a key element that financial examiners are looking to identify so credit holders interested in improving credit should always take measures to maintain a good image on paper. This can be executed by making the decision to limit the amount of personal credit cards open at once or, at the least, maintain low balances for each one; with all of them, not totaling more than provable income.

Of course, there are more ways to improve one's credit score, especially in the case of financial default on loans or monthly payments. Despite any damage done by failure to meet payment deadlines or accounts being closed, credit repair is as easy as re-establishing a positive credit report by repaying delinquent accounts and opening new accounts without negative marks.

One popular way to begin a more positive credit card history is to purchase a "secured credit card". In this case, one can just find any number of suitable secured credit cards online by doing a basic web search. Generally, these companies request the typical personal information including name, bank account information, and an initial deposit amount made online, in person, or by check via US mail. Using this type of credit card allows banks to provide you with the same types of bank card terms offered to the general public but with higher interest rates, but most importantly, by using these credit cards and then paying on them on time each month, ones credit is improved as the lending company reports your payments to one or all of the major financial profiling institutions.

Purchasing a longer term or installment loan is a traditional to improve on a credit score. This is the type of loan is important because for the lender, it that establishes a long term ability to make large payments, typically, for items such as a vehicle, mortgage or student loan. These types of loans compliment the other type of "revolving" or credit card loans. Paying off any type of installment loan can be beneficial in improving ones credit score says the loan payments are reported to all three major credit agencies.

Typically, paying off outdated bills that have fallen into collection is the road less traveled, but nonetheless, it serves as an equally effective method in improving ones credit rating. Failure to pay balances result in negative reports and marks, which can show up on your report from two years up to as long s 10 years. However, these negative reports can be amended with positive feedback after repayment. Although failure to pay on time may bring a score down, making good on the balance carries a lot of weight as it reinforces confidence that the person follows through on financial promises. These types of accounts are easily forgotten with time but still carry weight when it comes to your profile so it may be helpful to register with a credit report service that will allow you to monitor or sift through past accounts that may have been neglected.

Overall, learning how to improve your credit score requires taking steps to maintain the type of profile that showcases one with a low debt and revolving credit with long term history. At the opposite end of the scale, be sure to avoid the type of profile that reflects high debt with loads of revolving credit. This type of score is a red flag for financial overextension so be sure to allow yourself a comfortable cushion between the amount of credit you are allowed and the amount of credit you use.

About The Author

Darren Wiley has not only lived the life of someone who has had his finances out of control but also went on to get the necessary certification to be able to help others who are currently having problems keeping their finances in check as well. Truth be told, it is not a very arduous task to keep abreast of one's finances. The challenge comes in when things are allowed to accumulate and then there is a big pile of bills and other things to sort all at one time.

The aim that Darren has through this book is to guide the lost to a viable solution. It really is all about clearly the clutter in the financial aspect of one's life and then creating some sort of system to promote saving and also to ensure that the bills are paid on time.

Darren is also aware that not a lot of individuals like to speak about much less mention anything about finances but he has made put all his advice in a manner that it is easily understood by anyone that should opt to read this book. With proper planning you will be able to get those financial challenges sorted out, get your credit score in order and be able to borrow again if necessary.